An Animal Family

HORSES AND FOALS

By Emilia Hendrix

Gareth Stevens
PUBLISHING

Please visit our website, www.garethstevens.com. For a free color catalog of all our high-quality books, call toll free 1-800-542-2595 or fax 1-877-542-2596.

Cataloging-in-Publication Data

Hendrix, Emilia.
Horses and foals / by Emilia Hendrix.
p. cm. — (An animal family)
Includes index.
ISBN 978-1-4824-3775-1 (pbk.)
ISBN 978-1-4824-3776-8 (6-pack)
ISBN 978-1-4824-3777-5 (library binding)
1. Horses — Juvenile literature. I. Hendrix, Emilia. II. Title.
SF302.H46 2016
636.1—d23

First Edition

Published in 2016 by
Gareth Stevens Publishing
111 East 14th Street, Suite 349
New York, NY 10003

Editor: Ryan Nagelhout
Designer: Andrea Davison-Bartolotta

Photo credits: Cover, pp. 1, 21 Condor 36/Shutterstock.com; pp. 5, 19, 23 Zuzule/Shutterstock.com; p. 7 Alexey Stiop/Shutterstock.com; p. 9 Evgeny Dubinchuk/Shutterstock.com; pp. 11, 24 (foal) Anki Hoglund/Shutterstock.com; p. 13 DragoNika/Shutterstock.com; pp. 15, 24 (mare) Lenkadan/Shutterstock.com; p. 17 skmj/Shutterstock.com.

Printed in the United States of America

CPSIA compliance information: Batch #CW16GS: For further information contact Gareth Stevens, New York, New York at 1-800-542-2595.

Contents

Horses are fast animals.

Many live on farms.

Up to 20 wild horses live together.

Baby horses are foals.

Most babies are born in spring.

Mother horses
are mares.
They take care of
baby horses.

A boy horse is called
a colt.

A girl horse is called a filly.

Horses love to run!

They only eat plants.

Words to Know

foal

mare

Index